Shattered dreams

Marsha tore at the tissue, careful not to rip into the big "M." The box inside looked like the one her last year's winter boots had come in. When she opened it up, there inside the whispering tissue bulged the ugliest ice skates she had ever seen.

Author's Note

I wish to thank Pat Lewis and her second-grade children at Washington Elementary School and Jan Bishop and the first-graders of Springfield Elementary for hearing this story in its early stages in 1975. Because of their excitement I knew the story was working; because of their questions and comments, I made important changes. Thanks also to Sadie Penn, Lynn Reid Gray, and Barbara Lancaster Burise, who read the manuscript to their classes. I thank my husband, Jay, for falling asleep during a reading of my first, dull draft…and for his interest in my later version, which kept him reading over my shoulder to see what happened next. My fond appreciation to Tonya Hay for living the story when I read it to her in its nearly finished state, and to a very smart, sensitive lady—my editor, Jenny Frisse—who has lived with it in all its phases.

The Skates
of
Uncle Richard

Carol Fenner

illustrated by Ati Forberg

Harcourt Brace Jovanovich, Inc.
Orlando Austin San Diego Chicago Dallas New York

This book is for Grace Marie,
fellow dreamer...
one skate apiece
on Blueberry Hill,
saving
the doomed gardens, dreaming
the narrowest clubhouse
in Brooklyn

As a part of the HBJ TREASURY OF LITERATURE, 1993 Edition, this edition is published by special arrangement with Random House, Inc.

Grateful acknowledgment is made to Random House, Inc. for permission to reprint *The Skates of Uncle Richard* by Carol Fenner, illustrated by Ati Forberg. Text copyright © 1978 by Carol Fenner Williams; illustrations copyright © 1978 by Ati Forberg; cover illustration copyright © 1990 by Sheila Hamanaka.

Printed in the United States of America

ISBN 0-15-300339-1

2 3 4 5 6 7 8 9 10   059   96   95   94   93

Hold fast to dreams
For if dreams die
Life is a broken-winged bird
That cannot fly.

Hold fast to dreams
For when dreams go
Life is a barren field
Frozen with snow.

Langston Hughes

Marsha

Once there was an ice-skating champion, a beautiful black figure skater. She was tall and smooth and slender. She could swoop across the ice and leap into a double turn high in the middle of the air. She could spin so fast she could hardly be seen except for a whirling blur. She could also do a flying camel—a beautiful, slow spin on one leg, her body bent sideways into her reaching arms.

Her hair was braided into tight little ropes across her head, showing its fine shape. She had brown eyes that shone in a round, brown face. Her

9

picture was in the paper on the sports page. Television cameras followed her around while she skated so that people could watch her in their living rooms.

But there was only one person who knew where she lived. A girl named Marsha knew—because the beautiful black figure skater lived inside Marsha's head.

The big, gleaming skating arena lived in Marsha's head, too. And the music that was played. And the audience in the shadowy stands. And the television cameras.

Marsha was almost nine years old. She lived on a street lined with trees and big old houses. In front of each house was a square lawn full of grass in summer and leaves in the fall and snow in winter.

Marsha had a soft fluff of black hair and brown eyes that dreamed in a round, brown face. She was short and a little chubby. She was always dropping things or tripping over things because her mind was usually somewhere else.

She dreamed of discovering lost heroes and helping them home. She dreamed of mystery and finding clues and solving crimes. But, most of all, she dreamed of being a figure skater . . . tall and smooth and slender and able to spin and fly across the ice.

The ice skates of her dreams were snow-white with gleaming blades. They had red pompons, and little bells on the laces. On the front of the blades were little saw-toothed points, like little teeth. Marsha didn't know what the teeth were for, but she knew that they were important to a figure skater.

Marsha always wore a beautiful costume in her dream. Her favorite was a flying red skirt with fur around the bottom and a red sweater with hearts on the sleeves. She had as many outfits as she could dream up and she never worried about a closet big enough to keep them in.

There in the audience of her dream sat her mother, her mouth round with surprise. Sometimes her father, who had died when she was little, was there. His face was dim and smiling and he would clap his big hands gently to the music. Her older brother Leonard was always there feeling sorry he had ever called her "fatty."

They all watched as she skated in the silvery arena. She was tall and smooth and slender. She never missed a turn. She never moved out of step with the music. She never fell down.

In her wide-awake, real life, Marsha had been watching the championship skaters on television ever since she was six. She had seen blond German girls and red-cheeked Canadians. She had learned that the flying turn in the middle of the air was called an axel jump, and a double turn was a double axel. One year, there had been a Russian girl with a proud neck who did the best double axel. And once, a tiny American girl with freckles and bouncing hair won the gold medal. She did perfect figure eights and a breathtaking flying camel.

A part of Marsha always skated with the skaters she watched, seemed to breathe when they breathed. The only time she ever stood up to Leonard was when he once tried to change her skating program to the basketball game. She had been only seven at the time, and he had been so surprised he let her have her way.

Marsha had never seen a black skater on TV until the year she turned eight. Then, suddenly, there she was, whipping across the screen, a bold figure against the ice. Marsha's mouth had dropped. Then she had watched critically . . . as she had never watched the other skaters before. She would never forgive a stumble or a clumsy movement in this performer as she had excused others. But the black skater never faltered; she finished her piece with a slow, melting spin.

Marsha had let her breath out with the spin. Her dream was beating fiercely in her heart.

Marsha herself had never skated with real ice skates on real ice. Sometimes she skated without skates. She would stand alone in her room, her arms lifted in the empty air. She would bend forward and extend one leg behind. She could even imagine the coolness **drifting** up from the ice. But that was not nearly **as** satisfying as being the champion star skater **who** lived in her head.

Her older brother Leonard had ice skates with long, straight racing blades. He had mowed lawns one summer and bought them with the money he earned. Last winter, on one of his good-mood days, he had taken Marsha with him to the lagoon where everyone skated. Marsha had run and skidded about in her snow boots. But her legs had felt leaden and her heart couldn't soar. She felt miles away from being the beautiful skater of her dreams.

Summer came with all the long, warm days. Marsha turned nine. She learned how to swim. She rode on swings in the park. She helped her mother weed the garden. She played detective with her best friend. But Marsha's dream followed her into summer. At night, while the warm air drifted through her open window, she dreamed of ice-skating.

When the leaves began to change color, she grew excited at the thought of colder days and the lagoon freezing over. The dream followed her to school, and her mind would be far away when she was supposed to be thinking about numbers or the way words go together.

The days grew shorter and shorter. Then one day it snowed. Winter was really on its way. Thoughts of Christmas came into Marsha's dreaming head. She began to hint to her mother that she sure would like ice skates for Christmas this year.

"When you can watch where you're walking, maybe you can handle ice skates," her mother said. "When you can wipe the silverware without dropping it, maybe then . . ."

Marsha had never had a good reason before to watch where she walked or to keep hold of the silverware. She usually had more exciting things on her mind. But even if she tried hard to be more alert, Marsha didn't think she would ever get ice skates for Christmas. Her mother always seemed to get her things she thought Marsha should have, not things Marsha really wanted. One of her mother's favorite expressions was, "Money spent wisely lasts forever."

Marsha worried a little, too, about what would happen to the beautiful black skater in her head if the real Marsha ever got real ice skates on her real feet. Her dream skating, her leaps and spins, might not come true at all. Still she kept on hinting. And she tried really hard to watch where she walked. She didn't even drop the silverware any more. Her mother was pleasantly surprised.

Gradually, whenever Marsha brought up the subject of ice skates, her mother would look sort of thoughtful. Marsha's hopes rose. But her worry about losing the dream skater who lived in her head rose, too.

Thanksgiving came with its turkey and rolls, pumpkin pies and visitors.

Her mother complained about the stores getting all Christmas-y so soon.

Marsha made presents in her room, keeping the door closed and covering the keyhole against her peeking brother. Christmas Day came closer. She wrapped up the painting she had done for her mother and the papier-mâché box she had made for Leonard. She thought about ice skates with a terrible excitement and a little bit of dread.

Soon the houses on her block began to show Christmas tree lights in the windows. There were lights on some of the outdoor bushes, too. Marsha's mother always waited until just before Christmas to buy their tree. "When the price is right," she said firmly. Marsha and Leonard thought they would die of impatience before they finally got their own tree.

Two days before Christmas they visited the largest Christmas tree dealer in town. He still had a lot of trees left. "He's only got two days to sell them all," said their mother. "Pity we can't wait till after Christmas. He'd pay us to take one away." Both Marsha and Leonard cried out "After Christmas!" in such horrified voices that their mother burst out laughing.

They found a tree they liked, not too large, not too small. Their mother was happy to pay only two dollars. They took it home on their sled, singing "Jingle Bells" all the way. Even their mother sang with them.

They trimmed their tree with lights and tinsel, bright-colored balls, strings of homemade popcorn and cut-out paper angels. Marsha never dropped any of the lights or fragile balls or anything.

And now Christmas was nearly upon them. Leonard, who had crept about trying to locate hidden presents, began to wear a knowing smirk on his face. Marsha wondered if he'd seen her ice skates hidden somewhere. She didn't ask because she was afraid to know.

On Christmas morning, the first thing Marsha saw was her stocking, bulging with tangerines and pretty pencils. Then her eyes flew over the piles of packages to a large box covered with red tissue. It had silver stars pasted into the shape of her initial, a big starry "M." Her heart crowded into her throat.

She couldn't bring herself to open the red box right away. First she opened a flat box with a red-striped, homemade apron in it. She unwrapped a new plaid dress with a lace collar. There were two new books for her. But her mind was on the box covered with red tissue. She grew first hot, then cold, from excitement.

She opened a paint set she liked and a babydoll she didn't. There was a gift of warm underwear from Auntie Jess that her mother said she should be thankful for. Leonard gave her a flashlight, which he told her would keep her from tripping over her feet if she would keep it shining on them. Finally the present covered with red tissue was the only one left to open.

She tore at the tissue, careful not to rip into the big "M." The box inside looked like the one her last year's winter boots had come in. When she opened it up, there inside the whispering tissue bulged the ugliest ice skates she had ever seen.

For a while, Marsha just sat staring at the skates. Then dumbly she took them out of the box. They were old-fashioned hockey skates, black with brown leather around the thick toes and brown circles at the ankles. They had heavy, blunted blades, meant for charging, meant for stopping short and turning hard. They were not in the least the kind of skates for doing the flying camel or executing a perfect figure eight. And, although the blades were clean and shining, the skates had obviously been used and used and used before.

"They were your uncle Richard's," said her mother. "They were his skates when he was seven. He was about your size then. He kept them up real nice. They're almost good as new."

Marsha kept her eyes on the skates. Uncle Richard was old now . . . old, at least thirty. She could feel tears pushing to get out behind her eyes.

"Your uncle Richard is a fine skater," her mother continued. "He learned how to skate on those skates. They'll be a good start for you, Marsha, till we see how you take to skating."

Marsha sat on the floor with the box at her side, the ugly skates in her lap. "I remembered packing them away in the attic years ago," her mother was saying. "Richard'll be pleased to know they're being used." She added tartly, ". . . if he ever stops by long enough for a little conversation."

But Marsha was feeling the beautiful black skating champion inside her head disappear. The music and the arena were fading away. She was nine years old, a round and chubby little girl with no more wishes in her heart. Her dream had deserted her and the ugliest skates in the world lay in her plump little lap.

Uncle Richard

Marsha's uncle Richard was her mother's kid brother. But he was no longer a kid. He was thirty-one. He was very tall. He had a lime-green convertible and a lot of different girlfriends. Marsha's mother often bragged, "Richard can do anything he sets his mind to." She also complained that Richard didn't set his mind to anything for very long. He kept changing jobs and cars and girlfriends. "Richard is no longer a kid," said Marsha's mother, "but he still thinks he is."

27

Marsha didn't know her uncle very well. He didn't visit his folks much. And he never stayed around too long when he did drop by. But she admired how tall he was. She admired his beautiful black cloud of hair, his lime-green convertible, and the elegant clothes and hairstyles of the girlfriends he sometimes brought around. But it helped only a little knowing that those ugly, old, ugly, old ice skates had belonged to him.

After Christmas, the beautiful black skater never appeared whole and beautiful as before. Marsha stuffed Uncle Richard's skates way back in her closet, but it didn't help. If the dream skater came into Marsha's mind at all, she was short and chubby or her figure skates were too large or her nose was running or the ice would keep melting into water and she would fall in. Marsha couldn't get her dream together any more.

One Saturday morning, several weeks after Christmas vacation, she went to her closet and took out the ugly skates. She sat on her bed and tried them on. They were actually a pretty good fit. She stood up on them. They wobbled. Her ankles wobbled. She clutched the edge of the bed. "It's because there's no ice," she thought. "It'll be all right if there's ice."

At lunchtime she asked Leonard if he would take her to the lagoon. He made an annoyed face, but their mother saw. "Of course Leonard will take you, Marsha," she said, "and he'll help you, too, won't you, Leonard?" Leonard growled okay.

Later in the afternoon, however, he was in a better mood. It was a cold and shining day. "Perfect for skating," he announced, and Marsha felt a surge of hope.

When they reached the lagoon, there were many cars parked around it. All sizes of shoes and boots were scattered near the benches on the bank.

To Marsha they looked cold and lonely sitting in the snow. The little island in the middle of the lagoon was thick and shapeless with snow-fat trees and bushes. The ice all around it was alive with the activity of skaters, their shouts clear in the cold air. Marsha felt a shiver of fear nip and tremble in her stomach.

They sat on a cold bench to put on their skates. Leonard laced up rapidly, whistling. Then he stood up impatiently. He waved to some friends skating out on the lagoon. "Hurry up, will you?" he clucked fiercely at Marsha.

She finally got her skates laced to the top and tied. She stood up. Her feet didn't feel as if they could fly across the ice. They felt like blocks of wood. "Come on, Marsha," groaned Leonard. She took a step and the skates suddenly slipped away as if they were trying to escape from her feet. Up into the air went her legs. Down into the snow went Marsha.

"Oh, for cryin' out loud," wailed Leonard. But he helped her up and then down the bank to the ice. From a distance, the frozen lagoon had looked smooth. Close up, Marsha could see that the ice was pitted with the scars of many skates. There were ripples in it and bumps and some long, ragged cracks frozen over. Giggling nervously, Marsha stepped out onto the ice.

Whooooooooosh! Up into the air went Uncle Richard's skates. Down went Marsha onto the ice on her bottom. "Oh, for cryin' out loud," wailed Leonard again. He yanked her up by one arm. But her legs were going in different directions.

Whooooooooosh! Whooooooooosh! And down she went again. "Mar-sha!" complained Leonard. He helped her up again. "Now stand there," he commanded.

Wobbling and swaying, Marsha pushed into her ankles and stayed in one spot. Her arms were sticking out on either side, her ankles bent nearly double. She was practically standing on her ankles.

Leonard grabbed both of her hands. "Now," he ordered, "keep hold of my hands and keep your ankles straight, for cryin' out loud." Then, awkwardly, he began to skate backward, pulling Marsha forward. Her ankles caved in; her ankles bent out. Back and forth, in and out. She wobbled forward on the skates of Uncle Richard. Her head hunched down in front. Her bottom stuck out behind.

It was no fun. Leonard kept looking around for his friends. Marsha kept falling down. Her ankles began to ache dreadfully and her bottom was sore. Her nose was running. Finally Leonard dragged her to a bench near the little island and left her there. "Be right back," he said and skated away to talk with his friends.

Marsha sat on the bench alone. She fumbled for her handkerchief to blow her nose on. Her fingers were numb with cold. Tears of despair tickled behind her nose and clogged her head. She wanted to go home, but she didn't know how she would ever get back across the ice to the snow-bank where her boots sat. She dropped her head, full of cold and misery.

A scraping sound, ice skates stopping suddenly, made her look up. A man was standing in front of her, smiling. She was so wrapped up in unhappiness that at first she didn't know him. He was very tall and he had a long, red scarf that trailed over one shoulder. She saw he was leaning toward her, saying something, and she saw his beautiful black cloud of hair and then she recognized her uncle Richard.

He was saying, "Marsha girl, is that you? Why you lookin' so sad?" Marsha didn't know how to tell him, so she changed the subject. "Momma's mad at you again," she said shyly, "because you didn't come by on Christmas."

"Your momma is always mad at me," said Uncle Richard. He didn't sound too upset. "I was out of town," he added absently. Marsha saw he was looking at her skates. "Why don't you lace up your skates properly?" he asked. He bent way over and touched them thoughtfully. Marsha could see he was puzzled.

"They were your first skates when you were

seven," she explained in a low voice. Uncle Richard knelt down in front of her and took one of her feet in both of his hands. "Yeah," he whispered. "They sure are . . . they sure are. . . ." He looked up at her with delight growing in his face. "Those good old skates." He laughed. Then he began to undo the laces and Marsha thought he was going to take the skates back. But he was saying, "First off, Marsha, you've got to have your skates laced properly. Your feet are falling out of these. They're laced up all wrong."

Uncle Richard straightened the tongue in her

boot. He left the bottom lacings loose so she could wiggle her toes. Then he laced very tightly and evenly across her foot and above her ankle. He tied a knot and laced the rest loosely to the top of the boot. "How does that feel?" he asked after he'd done both feet. It felt great. Like brand-new ankles.

Then he stood her up and began to pull her slowly and evenly across the ice. "Bend your knees, not your middle," he told her. Marsha bent her knees and her middle straightened right up. She was surprised at how easily she could balance now.

After they had gone a short distance, Uncle Richard said, "You do that real easy, so I want to show you some things to practice here while I get some skating done." First he showed Marsha how to rest her ankles when they got tired. "Stand quiet," he said, "and let your ankles relax right down into your boots . . . right down into the ice. That's important."

Then he said, "Here's something else to practice. Watch close." He pushed forward into one foot and trailed the other behind lightly without touching the ice. "Just bend your knee and lean into it," he said, "nice and easy."

Then he brought the other foot forward and pushed easily into that one. "I push," he said, "and then I glide . . . and then I push with the other foot. And then I glide!" Uncle Richard glided forward, first on one foot and then the other. "Push, glide . . . push, glide. Get it?" Marsha nodded. It made good sense.

"Now you practice that for a while. Practice resting your ankles, too, whenever they get tired. Okay?" Marsha nodded and Uncle Richard skated off, his red scarf trailing. She watched to see if he really could skate as well as her mother said.

Slowly at first Uncle Richard moved across the ice. Then Marsha saw him reach into his pocket and pull out a tiny radio. He held it next to his ear and began to skate to music no one else could hear. Marsha noticed he glided a long time on one foot before he shifted his weight to the other one.

Then he made some smooth, neat turns. His speed quickened. He circled into a spin that blurred his entire outline. The red scarf whipped around him and, as the spin slowed down, gradually began to unwind.

"Oh," breathed Marsha. "Oh, he is fine. He is really fine." Her uncle began skating backward, leaning his ear into the hand that held the radio. He seemed to be sailing, led backward by the music around the lagoon. He never tripped over the humps and cracks in the ice.

People began to stop skating and watch Uncle Richard, who now turned and sped forward. Suddenly he swooped and leapt into a single axel, fine as any Olympic skater. He circled to a halt and began to skate backward again, disappearing around a bend in the little island.

Alone in the middle of the ice, Marsha felt her ankles begin to wobble with worry. She tried

resting them. It worked. They stopped wobbling. "But I can't stand here forever," she thought. She tested herself, lifting first one foot and then the other. She took a few timid steps. She skidded a little. She glided a little. She stopped and rested.

Then she took a deep breath, bent her knee, and pushed off into her right foot the way Uncle Richard had done. She glided a little, her body balanced over her skating foot. Then she shifted and pushed into her left foot and glided a shaky distance. It worked! Push, glide . . . push, glide. She brought her legs together and glided on both feet all by herself out alone in the middle of the ice.

She gasped with excitement. It was fun! She tried it again. She pushed off more boldly and glided farther. She did it over again. And again. After a while she rested her ankles. Then she practiced some more . . . push, glide . . . push, glide. She watched her feet. She tried to glide longer on one foot. Push, glide . . . push, glide. She tried to keep her knees bent, her middle straight. Push, glide . . . push, glide.

Suddenly she realized she was at the other end

of the lagoon. "My, MY," said a voice behind her. "I thought I left you down at the other end." It was Uncle Richard. He was turning off his radio and smiling. "How'd you get here?" he asked.

"I push-push-glided," said Marsha. "All by myself. No one helped."

"You foolin' me?" asked Uncle Richard, smiling. "Let's see!"

Wobbling only a little at the beginning, Marsha performed her push, glide . . . push, glide. She remembered to keep her skating knee bent. She skated in a medium-sized circle around him and stopped.

"You are one surprising young lady," said Uncle Richard. "You sure learn fast." Marsha was surprised herself. He bent down and looked seriously into her face. "You ready for another suggestion?" he asked.

Marsha felt, in that moment, that Uncle Richard could see inside her heart better than anyone. The beautiful figure skater of her dreams floated briefly into her mind, but Marsha didn't have time for her now.

"I want to learn how to skate like you skate," she said. Her voice sounded so little and low to her that she wondered if he'd heard her. But Uncle Richard touched her cheek softly with his fingertips. He looked very thoughtful for a minute. Then he said quietly, "Okay. We'll work on it."

He stood up. "First off, don't leave your body all bundled down inside your coat. Don't watch your feet. Stretch up. Be proud. But not stiff. Look where you're going. Reach after the sky . . . or the moon . . . or a treetop. Okay? You hear? You remember that?" Marsha nodded, her heart pounding.

"You're a natural," said Uncle Richard. "You can be a super fine skater. But you'll have to set your mind to it." Marsha nodded again. She understood. Uncle Richard suddenly laughed out loud. "We'll surprise your momma. Maybe we'll shake up the whole world, okay?" he asked.

"Okay," she said, feeling very warm and sure.

"Now you keep practicing," said Uncle Richard. "Next week we'll have another lesson. I'll talk to your momma. Maybe she'll like me again, okay?" Marsha beamed at him. "They're a good old pair of skates. Oil the runners, you hear?" Marsha nodded.

Uncle Richard pushed off. She watched him glide away. Other people watched him, too. He turned up the radio again and held it to his ear. It was as if he'd gone through an invisible door onto another winter lagoon that belonged only to him.

Marsha pushed off after him, her head riding high, her round little body stretched taller . . . reaching after him, after the sky or the moon or the tops of the trees. Push, glide . . . push, glide. Past her staring brother she skated. Hardly even a wobble. Proud, not stiff. She glided away on the skates of Uncle Richard, taller and taller and taller, never once falling down.